W9-CCF-927

Kids Can Do It!

I CAN START A BAND!

by Ruth Owen

WINDMILL
BOOKS ™

Published in 2018 by **Windmill Books**, an Imprint of Rosen Publishing
29 East 21st Street, New York, NY 10010

Produced for Rosen by Ruby Tuesday Books Ltd
Designer: Tammy West

Photo Credits: Courtesy of Ruby Tuesday Books and Shutterstock.

Cataloging-in-Publication Data
Names: Owen, Ruth.
Title: I can start a band! / Ruth Owen.
Description: New York : Windmill Books, 2018. | Series: Kids can do it! | Includes index.
Identifiers: ISBN 9781499483536 (pbk.) | ISBN 9781499483475 (library bound) |
   ISBN 9781499483369 (6 pack)
Subjects: LCSH: Bands (Music)--Juvenile literature. | Rock music--Juvenile literature.
Classification: LCC ML3795.094 2018 | DDC 781.64023--dc23

Manufactured in the United States of America
CPSIA Compliance Information: Batch BS17WM: For Further Information contact Rosen Publishing, New York, New York at 1-800-237-9932

WARNING:

Some of the activities in this book require adult help.
It's also important that all laws and regulations are followed when carrying
out the activities in this book. The author and publisher disclaim any liability
in connection with the use of the information in this book.

CONTENTS

LOVE MUSIC?
START A BAND!

Do you find yourself singing and humming as you go about your day? Maybe as you're doing your homework, your hands are constantly tapping out a rhythm on the tabletop?

If you can't wait to play your guitar after school, or you're never without your headphones, then music is in your blood.

Playing music or writing songs on your own can be a fun hobby. Sharing your music with others can be even more enjoyable. Maybe it's time to start your own band?

This book is an introduction to some of the things you'll need to think about when starting a band. Get to know the basics, and then get creating new music!

If you go online, you'll find thousands of bands and **artists** sharing and promoting their music. What will make your band unique and successful?

DO YOUR MUSIC RESEARCH

If you love music, take every opportunity to see bands play live and check out what other musicians are doing.

Go to local festivals and other events where you will get the chance to see bands perform.

Listen to lots of music from the past. A song may be 50 years old, but it might **inspire** you to create something of your own.

Go online to find new bands and artists. Follow them on social media to learn what they're doing and to discover who they are listening to and following.

You may have a favorite type of music, but experiment by listening to other music **genres**. Set yourself a challenge: listen to and learn about a different music genre each week. You'll have lots of fun discovering new sounds.

Folk

Dance

Blues

Reggae

POP

Hip-hop

Jazz

Punk

Classical

Rock

Heavy metal

Country

DISCO

WHAT TYPE OF BAND?

There are many different types of bands playing a wide variety of music genres.

Will your band play rock, pop, or country music? Maybe your sound will be a **fusion** of different genres.

Maybe you love punk from the 1970s and rock music. One of your band members, however, plays the piano and is passionate about classical music. Together you can have lots of fun mixing up these different types of music and creating something entirely new. It's your band—so find your own sound!

A band might be a combination of a lead singer, or vocalist, a guitarist and **bass guitarist** playing **electric guitars**, and a drummer. Maybe there will also be a band member who plays keyboards. A band might also be just two vocalists playing **acoustic guitars**. What instruments will be in your band?

Here are some of the instruments and pieces of equipment you might need for your band.

A microphone

A keyboard can be played like a piano. It can also make the sounds of other instruments and many different noises and effects.

Electric guitar

Amplifier

Drum kit

An electric guitar and amplifier (amp). An amp is a device that makes sounds louder.

If you don't have everything at first, that's fine. Get practicing with what you do have and over time, build up your collection of instruments and equipment.

Acoustic guitar

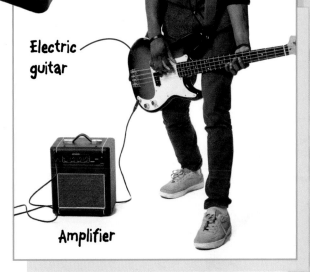

PUTTING THE BAND TOGETHER

Once you've decided to start a band, you'll need band members.

You might have friends, siblings, or cousins who want to join your band. If you're a member of a choir or music club, put the word out that you're looking for other singers or musicians to join you.

You can also hold **auditions** to find band members. At an audition, prospective band members will sing or play an instrument to show you what they can do.

It's helpful if members of a band have other skills, too.

A band member with artistic skills can help design posters, costumes, and (maybe one day) album covers.

A band member with good computer skills will be helpful when you're all learning and using new apps and software for recording your music or making videos.

When you're ready, your band can use social media to promote its music. Who will be in charge of tweeting, posting on Instagram, and updating the band's Facebook page and website?

1 Choose a place to hold your audition. Maybe you can use a music room at school? You could hold the audition in a garage or basement—any place where you can make some noise and not disturb your family or neighbors.

2 You can audition singers and musicians on the same day, or just focus on finding one band member at a time.

3 Decide when the audition will be, and then put up a poster on your school bulletin board.

4 On the day of the audition, ask any existing band members or a couple of friends to come along to give their opinion on the candidates.

GUITARIST WANTED

for a new rock band

Must have own guitar

Auditions will be held on Saturday May 6th

For more details speak to Sam Parker

NAMING THE BAND

Once you've formed the band, it's time to think of a name!

If you don't already have a name in mind, there are lots of fun ways to get started.

Try thinking of nouns, like cell phone, planet, and rattlesnake. Then make the nouns plural and add "The" to get: The Cell Phones, The Planets, The Rattlesnakes.

You can then take this idea one step further by adding a descriptive word: The Silver Cell Phones, The Black Planets, The Burning Rattlesnakes.

What band names do you like? Go online and research the origin of the name. How did the band choose it and why?

Try putting together rhyming words: The Tiger Spiders, The Red Freds, Zinc Pink. If what you come up with is nonsense, that's no problem!

1 If you get stuck, ask everyone to write five nouns and five adjectives on scraps of paper. Add some pet names, favorite colors or foods, and the names of characters from books, TV shows, and movies.

Put all the pieces of paper in a bowl, mix them up, and pull them out two at a time. You might accidentally discover a winning combination or at least get some fresh inspiration.

You can find fun band name generators online. These websites get you to fill in words and ideas and then generate random band names for you.

Red
Minions
DYLAN
Banana
PINK
Star
TAYLOR
Rat
Ice Cream
BASEBALL
BLUE
Jaws
Burning
Sneaker
Drum
Felix

IT'S ALL ABOUT TEAMWORK

Once the whole band has agreed on a name, check online that no other bands are using that name, or have a name that's very similar. If you're going to set up your own website, ask an adult to help you register and buy the domain name for your band.

STYLING YOUR BAND

You've found your band members and you've decided on a name and the type of music you'll play. Now it's time to think about your band's look.

What clothes will the band wear when you perform? Will you look dressed up or casual, glamorous or grungy? You don't all have to wear exactly the same outfit, but maybe you'll all wear jeans and sneakers, or all wear black.

Putting together a look for your band doesn't have to be expensive.

How will your band's name appear online and on posters? Using a computer or drawing by hand, create a logo for your band that fans can instantly recognize.

DARK WARRIOR

Once the band is online, you'll want to post lots of photos. Take casual behind-the-scenes photos of the band rehearsing and having fun. Also, pose for photos that show off your look.

Try designing an album cover. What photo will you choose? Try using Photoshop effects and experiment with your band's name and logo.

WRITING SONGS

If you're thinking of starting a band, you may have already begun writing songs. Once you have bandmates to work with, you can develop ideas together.

There are four main parts to writing a song:
- The inspiration, or idea
- The melody (or tune)
- The lyrics (or words)
- The structure of the song

A song can get started in lots of different ways. Some lyrics might pop into your head while you're watching a movie. You might wake up with a melody running through your mind from a dream. Grab it and build on it. The smallest idea could develop into an awesome song.

Just go for it! Have fun and don't try to judge whether your song is good or bad.

If you find writing songs hard, don't worry. As your experience grows, your songs will get better.

Always carry a notebook for jotting down ideas and scraps of lyrics. Everything around you can become an inspiration for the words in a song.

To write a song, you need an idea or subject. Sometimes just a feeling can be the inspiration behind a song.

Most songs are about love – the joy of loving someone or the heartbreak when the relationship ends. Many artists write entire albums about a break-up or an ex!

When someone you love dies, like a grandparent, friend, or pet, your feelings of grief can be poured into the words of a song.

A song can also be just a simple expression of joy! Write about how good it feels to dance, clap your hands, or laugh with friends.

Some songs are written about important issues around the world. Your passion for protecting wildlife or a desire to help homeless people could become a powerful song that many people will relate to.

A song's melody can come from anywhere!

You might suddenly find yourself humming something and realize it's a completely original tune.

You could be playing around with sounds on your instrument or jamming with friends when you find a melody.

Listen to sounds around you. A vacuum cleaner, a cat's purr, rain beating on the roof, or stamping feet could all inspire a beat or sound.

When you're working on a melody, you don't have to stick to the musical notes that you learned in a music class. Experiment with your instruments and your voice.

Sounds don't only have to come from musical instruments. Bang things and shake them. If you like the sound, include it in your song.

Just like finding your own melody, there are no rules when it comes to writing lyrics.

The lyrics of your song might tell a story with a beginning, middle, and end. Everyone who listens to the song will understand what it's about.

A song's lyrics can directly rhyme:

Every night I look at the moon,
and hope that you'll be home soon.

Or the lyrics can almost rhyme:

Every night I look at the moon,
I close my eyes and dream of you.

Alternatively, your lyrics might be more **cryptic**, like a poem. This means it might be hard for listeners to know exactly what you're saying. Everyone who listens to the song may find their own meaning in your words.

You can write all the lyrics for a song even if you don't have a melody. Or you may start out with a melody, and then write some lyrics to fit that tune.

THE STRUCTURE OF A SONG

Your song is your work, so you can arrange the parts of the song in any way you want. Many songs, however, are written using the following structure.

The First Verse

The first verse draws the listener in to the song's melody, and the song's "story" begins. As you listen to this verse, there's a sense of the song building up to the chorus.

The Chorus

This is the catchiest part of the song. The music may get louder with more instruments joining in. The lyrics are repetitive and tell the listener what the main idea of the song is all about.

The Second Verse

The lyrics pick up the story of the song again, and the music goes back to the original melody.

The Chorus

Once again, the music becomes more dynamic, and the lyrics are repeated.

The Bridge

At this point in the song, a new melody is introduced. The music may become slower or the singer may change key. This is the moment in the song where the listener might find out how the story ends, or the ideas explored in the verses come together in a way that gives the listener goosebumps.

The melody and the singer's voice may build and build into the final chorus.

The Final Chorus

This is the song's finale! The chorus may be repeated two, three, or four times. More instruments might join in.

The singer might do something different with their voice to bring the song to an earth-shaking, dramatic ending. Or the song may softly die and fade away, leaving the listener wanting more!

BAND REHEARSALS

Don't worry if your band doesn't sound great at first. All the artists you love to listen to were once at the start of their music careers, too. Make sure that the band rehearses regularly, and your skills will soon improve.

Find a rehearsal space. A garage, basement, or community hall are all good options. You can even rehearse in your bedroom.

Until you've written some songs of your own, learn to play other artists' songs. This will give you a chance to practice playing and performing as a band.

Make a plan for each rehearsal so you don't waste time. Maybe learn a **cover** one week and work on songwriting the next.

Get ready to perform. For example, will there be dancing or movement around the stage? Will the vocalist and guitarist sing together during the chorus?

If you've only performed alone in front of your bedroom mirror, you might feel shy at first, but that's what rehearsal time is for!

Make sure you plan what you'll do next time you meet. Then send everyone home with new songs to learn or songs to practice, so you'll all be ready for the next rehearsal.

Maybe you'll want to improve your own musical skills or learn to play a completely new instrument? One way to learn is to take lessons with an experienced teacher. Maybe an older friend or relative who plays will help you get started. You can also watch YouTube videos that will help teach you how to play the guitar and other instruments.

RECORDING YOUR SONGS

In the past, once a band had some songs they wanted to record, they had to play in a recording studio filled with expensive equipment.

Today, it's possible to record music using just a few pieces of equipment and a laptop. In fact, you can turn your bedroom into a recording studio!

When your band is ready to start recording music, you can buy a setup that includes microphones and a device called a digital audio interface.

A digital audio interface

The band's microphones, electric guitars, and keyboards are plugged into the digital audio interface. Then this device is connected to a laptop. The digital audio interface converts the recorded sound into digital data that goes to the laptop.

Once the music is on a laptop, a band can use computer software to work on their song until it's ready to be shared online or put onto a CD.

GarageBand is an app that bands can use to record music using tablets or laptops. The app allows the user to record live instruments and vocals, or combine a singer's voice with virtual instruments.

MAKE A VIDEO

Once you're writing and recording songs, why not try making a video?

1 Choose your best song to perform in the video. Ask your friends and family members for their opinion on which song is the band's strongest.

2 To make the recording, you'll need a video camera, or a smartphone or tablet with recording capabilities. If you don't have a way to do this, borrow the equipment you need.

3 Create your video's concept. Will the video show a live performance? Perhaps your idea is to act out the song's story.

4 Choose the location where you will record the video. Depending on the story behind your song or your band's music genre, you might want to record in a location such as a spooky forest or outside a grungy, abandoned building.

Camcorder

Abandoned buildings on a city street can become a filming location. Make sure you have an adult's permission before you go exploring.

In a dark bedroom, strings of colored lights will create atmosphere.

5 Experiment with camera angles. Maybe you want to zoom in on the guitarist's hands, or shoot the vocalist from one side or another.

6 Once you've planned the story and concept behind the video, rehearse the performance. Then get recording!

New equipment, software, and apps are created all the time. Keep researching what's available for recording music and making videos. Many great options are free or fairly cheap.

7 Film the video three or four times. This will give you lots of options once you're ready to **edit** your recordings. Editing the video means piecing together segments containing music and action from the different recordings to get the best version of your performance.

8 Many computers have software for editing videos. There are also many editing programs available to buy or download for free online. Teach yourself how to use this software and then get creative with the material you've recorded.

Add special effects to your video.

SHOWCASE YOUR BAND

Once your band can perform about 10 songs, you might feel ready to do a live performance and showcase the band.

A small event, such as a family party, is an ideal opportunity to perform your first gig.

Another good option is a school concert. You can use the school's equipment and lights, and get help from your teachers to set up your gear and rehearse.

When you feel ready, you might get the chance to perform at a local event, such as a street fair.

Ask your friends and family which songs are your strongest and then practice and perform those numbers.

Make sure that a helper films your live performance. You might want to use it in future videos or post songs from your show online.

Ask your family and friends for an honest opinion. Is the band good enough to perform live? It can be tough to get criticism, but listen and take the comments. Remember! People who care about you only want you to succeed.

GET YOUR MUSIC OUT THERE

You've got songs, recordings, and videos. Now it's time to get your band online and start building your fan base!

You can build and design a website for the band. There are lots of options online that will take you step-by-step through creating a website. And they're free!

Visit the YouTube channels and websites of other young artists to get ideas for promoting your band. Follow them, and they might follow you!

Build a social media profile by setting up a Facebook page, using Twitter, and posting pictures on Instagram and other sites.

Once you have professional-looking videos, you can set up a YouTube channel and upload your videos. Depending on your age, you might need an adult to set up the account for you.

What can you put online? Photos, videos, snippets of lyrics, and information about forthcoming gigs. Talk about music, and tell your followers who you are listening to.

IT'S ALL ABOUT TEAMWORK

Before you set up a website, use social media, or upload videos to YouTube, ask an adult for permission. Talk about your plans for promoting the band with the adults who take care of you. Ask for their help to get your plans underway, and never put material online without showing an adult first.

You might not have millions of followers like your favorite artists, but keep promoting your work and build slowly.

Your first band is all about learning and getting experience. Keep writing songs, keep practicing, and above all else, make sure you have LOTS OF FUN!

GLOSSARY

acoustic guitars
Guitars that produce sound by transmitting the vibrations of the strings into the air, as opposed to using electricity to amplify the sound.

artists
Singers and musicians.

auditions
Interviews for a job as a singer, musician, dancer, or actor.

bass guitarist
A musician who plays bass guitar. This type of guitar has a low sound and provides a connection between a band's drums and the other guitars. The bass guitarist helps to set a song's rhythm.

cover
A version of someone else's song.

cryptic
Having a meaning that is mysterious or obscure.

edit
To prepare a video or film by rearranging, deleting, or adding sections.

electric guitars
Guitars that need electricity to make sound. An electric guitar has parts called pickups that convert string vibrations into electrical signals to be amplified.

fusion
A combination of two or more different things.

genres
Styles or types of music, movies, or books. Rock, punk, and heavy metal are all music genres.

inspire
To fill someone with the urge to do something or create something.

WEBSITES

For web resources related to the subject of this book, go to:
www.windmillbooks.com/weblinks and select this book's title.

INDEX